THE WESTON CLEVEDON & PORTISHEAD RAILWAY
A PICTORIAL RECC

Peter Strange

Ex-Southern Railway 'Terrier' No. 2 *Portishead* with Weston to Clevedon train crossing the bridge over the River Yeo at Wick St. Lawrence on Whitsun Bank Holiday Monday, 6 June 1938. Note the high tide.

No. 1 *Clevedon* leaving Clevedon Gas Works in September 1937.

British Library Cataloguing in Publication Data
The Weston, Clevedon & Portishead Railway:
a pictorial record.
1. Avon. Railway services, history
I. Strange, Peter
385′.09423′9

TWELVEHEADS PRESS

**First published 1989 by Twelveheads Press,
Chy Mengleth, Twelveheads,
Truro, Cornwall TR4 8SN.**

ISBN 0 906294 19 3

PREFACE

In 1936, I was living in Clevedon and being interested in railways and photography it was only natural that I should turn my attention to the 'local line'. Many of the smaller and independent railways at that time were being forced to close, largely due to the increasing competition from road transport. I refer in particular to such lines as the Lynton & Barnstaple, Bishops Castle, Southwold, Selsey Tramway, Leek & Manifold, and numerous narrow gauge railways throughout the United Kingdom. I concluded that it would not be long before the Weston, Clevedon & Portishead Railway would suffer a similar fate and this encouraged me to amass as much material as I could to create a permanent record of this interesting railway so that, at the age of 15, I started taking photographs of the WC&PR and collecting other material that was available.

It was indeed fortunate that there were a number of members of the railway's original staff still alive in Clevedon and from whom I was able to obtain many photographs taken in the earliest days of the line's operation. These pictures provide a unique record of locomotives and trains of the time and in one particular case reveal the existence of a hitherto unknown locomotive.

I was especially indebted to Mr George Hancock of Clevedon, who was one of the first drivers to be employed by the Company and who appears in many of the early photographs. Also to Mr J. H. P. Capell, whose father was a Weston-super-Mare solicitor who sold to the railway the land on which the Ashcombe Road terminus was constructed, and who was a railway enthusiast himself. I also have to thank a local professional photographer by the name of Edwin H. Hazell who, knowing of my interest in the railway, gave me his collection of glass negatives of photographs which he had taken during 1920–21. Mr Hazell was commissioned by the railway to photograph the line in its entirety for litigation purposes following an accident involving some cattle near Kingston Road.

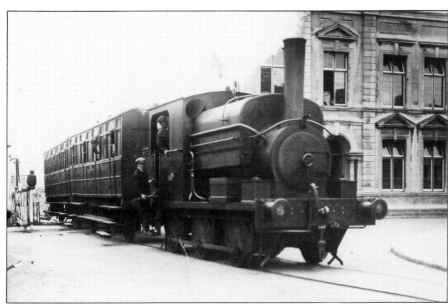

No.5 crossing Clevedon Triangle on 16 July 1925 with a train from Portishead.

Although regarded by many as something of a local joke, the railway was, in fact, efficiently run by an enthusiastic and friendly staff. It provided a most useful service for Clevedon commuters and school children making regular daily trips to and from Weston-super-Mare. The line boasted 'the shortest and quickest route to Weston-super-Mare' . . . a situation not improved upon until the opening of the M5 motorway some forty years later. The direct route to Weston by WC&PR was just over eight miles, whilst the distance by road through Yatton and Congresbury was sixteen. Furthermore, if one travelled by the GWR this was also time consuming and required a change of trains at Yatton. WC&PR trains generally ran to time, although breakdowns occurred occasionally.

Traffic between Clevedon and Portishead was very mixed, with fewer passengers being carried. The main function of this section was to service the vari-ous quarries en route, together with conveying coal to the Clevedon Gas Company. Portishead was also the main connecting point with the GWR and although the link with the latter at Clevedon was still in situ until the early thirties it was not used after 1908.

The object of this publication is to provide a pictorial history of one of the more unusual and interesting independent railways which existed prior to World War II. In order to provide a complete record and because of the scarcity of certain material, it has been necessary to repeat some photographs which have appeared in previous publications, but wherever possible hitherto unpublished material has been used. The photographs of locomotives and rolling stock have been reproduced in chronological order and those of station and track scenes in geographical sequence commencing at Weston-super-Mare.

August Bank Holiday crowd at Ashcombe Road station, Weston-super-Mare, in 1927.

HISTORICAL BACKGROUND

On 20 December 1884 the Weston-super-Mare, Clevedon, and Portishead Tramways Bill was deposited with Parliament and the Act received the Royal Assent on 6 August 1885. The tramway was to be of standard gauge.

Work commenced on the construction of the Weston to Clevedon section in 1888 but mainly due to financial and other problems this section was not completed until 1897. Following trial runs in the summer of that year the first scheduled sevices commenced on 1 December. It was originally intended to extend the tramway from its terminus in Ashcombe Road along the public streets of Weston-super-Mare to terminate in the Boulevard. Although some of the track was actually laid this section was never completed and that which had been laid was subsequently removed.

A further Act of Parliament dated 9 August 1899 authorised the conversion of the 'tramway' to a light railway. It also permitted the change of name to the Weston, Clevedon & Portishead Light Railway Company.

During the period up to 1897 plans were being made for the extension of the line to Portishead. Here again similar financial problems occurred and a further ten years elapsed before the first train ran on 7 August 1907. In 1905 it was apparent that the railway was in serious financial trouble. Further funds were obtained from various sources including the Excess Insurance Company, who, being the principal creditor, took the Company into receivership in 1909 and became its new proprietors.

In 1911 H. F. Stephens took over the management of the WC&PR and administered it from his office at Tonbridge in Kent. Stephens became known as the 'light railway king' because of his involvement in several other similar railways. Various schemes for extending the line to other locations came to nothing, with the exception of one for the construction of a wharf on the River Yeo at Wick St. Lawrence. This was completed in 1915 but was not used much, if at all, until after the first World War. This facility was mainly used for the importation of coal from

The small railcar at Weston, 22 May 1933.

South Wales, which was cheaper and more direct than via the GWR to Clevedon. Most of the Company's locomotive fuel was brought in by this direct route. During the early 1920s Stephens, being an innovative man, acquired two ketches, named the *Sarah* and the *Lily*, for this purpose. This venture proved entirely uneconomic. On one trip to Wick St. Lawrence with a load of coal from South Wales the *Lily* foundered off the coast near Newport and went to the bottom. The crew were fortunately saved. Another similar boat named the *Edith* and owned by a local firm of coal merchants was a regular visitor during the latter years and a photograph of her discharging her cargo appears in this album.

The railway was noted for its unusual collection of locomotives and rolling stock. The Company purchased only two new locomotives during its 42 years of operation, namely the Hudswell Clarke 0-6-0 saddle tank *Walton Park* in 1908 and the Manning Wardle 0-6-0 saddle tank *No. 5* in 1919. All remaining locomotives were acquired second hand (in some cases third, fourth or even fifth hand) from various sources. The original six American style bogie coaches, although delivered 'new', were in fact a frustrated export order originally intended for a South American railway (hence the design) and obviously bought at some advantageous price. After the Portishead extension was opened in 1907 the Company obtained a variety of four-wheeled coaches from various sources such as the Metropolitan Railway, the London & South Western Railway and the Taff Vale Railway.

In 1921 the Company purchased from the Drewry Car Co. Ltd. a four-wheeled petrol driven railcar which was succeeded by a further larger vehicle made by the same firm for the Southern Railway and purchased from the latter in 1934. In addition to the former the Company also acquired new a four-wheeled petrol driven tractor built by Muir Hill Fordson, closely followed by another, the first being written off following an accident. The purpose of these tractors was shunting on the jetty at Wick St. Lawrence, where weight restrictions prevented the use of the steam locomotives. The Company also owned a variety of open wagons, a four-wheel brake

van acquired from the Great Eastern Railway and an ex-Midland Railway brake van.

The Company's financial state fluctuated considerably. It showed a small profit during some of the years up to the outbreak of World War I and again during the early 1920s, mainly due to the more economic use of railcar services. Otherwise it showed a steady decline until the end when the maximum loss was sustained during the final months after the outbreak of World War II. The Company relied on a large proportion of its revenue from the conveyance of limestone from the Black Rock quarries near Portishead and the decline of this traffic, due to competition from road transport, no doubt contributed largely to the railway's demise.

Colonel Stephens (he gained the rank during the War) died in 1931 and his position was filled by his engineering assistant, Mr W. H. Austen, who remained in control until the end. From this time until the closure in 1940 the railway's fortunes declined and many problems occurred to make its existence very tenuous. The Railway Control Order of 1 September 1939 vesting control of the country's main line systems in the Ministry of Transport did not apply to the WC&PR and it was obliged to try and continue functioning as in the past. Losses continued to mount and notwithstanding reductions in services it was compelled to apply for a Court Order to close the line, doing so on 18 May 1940. Many of the staff employed at the time were taken on by the GWR and the Company tried to have the line adopted by the Railway Executive but to no avail.

The export of coal to the European continent ceased after the capitulation of France and consequently extra storage sidings were needed. The Ministry of Transport approved the WC&PR for this purpose and the GWR agreed to purchase the line from the Excess Insurance Company for £10,000. The transfer took effect from 22 June 1940 but the acquisition did not include the ownership of the land. The line was never actually used for the storage of coal. On 21 August all the railway's rolling stock, excluding locomotives, was formed into two trains and taken to Swindon. The locomotives – No. 1 *Clevedon* and the two Stroudley Terriers – were towed up separately,

No. 2 *Portishead* with ex-Taff Vale coach arriving at Clevedon from Portishead in May 1938.

No. 1 being subsequently scrapped and the Terriers taken into GWR stock and numbered 5 and 6 respectively. The total stock, excluding the two Terriers, was condemned. Many of the coach bodies were sold for various purposes and by chance the single ex-Metropolitan coach no. 7 has now found its way into the hands of the Metropolitan Society where it is being refurbished.

The Terriers were repainted by the GWR in their austerity green and No. 5 (WC&PR No. 2 *Portishead*) was returned to Clevedon in September 1940 where it remained on shed for a short period. It was photographed by the GWR in this location on 18 September 1940.

After some period of indecision it was decided to remove all the track and any other material which would be of benefit to the War effort. Work on the removal of the track commenced at Weston on 3 October 1942 and proceeded in the direction of Portishead, being completed in June 1943. Due to inaccessibility a section of track from the Clevedon side of the bridge over the River Yeo at Wick St. Lawrence to Ebdon Lane remained in situ until late 1943.

As the rails had been manufactured originally by Krupp of Essen much publicity was made of the fact that the raw material was now being returned to its country of origin with the compliments of RAF Bomber Command!

Although the railway's lands were vested in the statutory company, the Company itself having no title deeds, officers or Common Seal, ceased to exist. After receiving no response to notices served on the general public by the local authority, squatters eventually moved in and annexed various sections of the land.

Few visible signs of the railway exist today except for the steelwork of a bridge near Portishead and the remains of the bridge supports and wharf at Wick St. Lawrence. The museum at Weston-super-Mare has a light railway exhibit which includes one of the nameplates from the locomotive *Hesperus*. The Bristol Railway Circle also possesses one of the original brass nameplates of the single-wheeler *Clevedon* and one of the nameplates from the last *Weston*.

The *Harold* was built by Kitson in 1872 and was hired from Mackay & Davies of South Wales for the initial services of the WC&PR. Numbered 45 by the hirers this engine was painted bright scarlet. The *Harold* did not remain on the line long and was soon replaced by the first *Clevedon*. Depicted in the photograph on the first official day, 1 December 1897, at Clevedon, are Mr E. R. Wintour, traffic manager, standing at front of engine, driver Jack Jones on the footplate and George Hancock by the rear buffer beam. Initial trial runs were carried out during the summer of 1897 and it is possible that this locomotive was used for this purpose although there is no substantive information to this effect.

Author's Collection

The first *Clevedon* at Clevedon station in early 1898. The existence of this locomotive was unknown by the author until this photograph was procured from George Hancock of Clevedon, one of the first drivers employed by the company. Built by Walker Brothers of Wigan it was an 0-6-0 side tank with 13" x 20" inside cylinders and 3' 3" wheels. Prior to the opening of the Portishead extension in 1907 it was necessary to make a connection with the GWR at Clevedon via a very tight radius curve situated at the rear of the locomotive shed. In order to negotiate this sharp curve one pair of connecting rods on most six coupled locomotives was removed. This photograph shows *Clevedon* running in this manner. This engine was only in service for approximately six months, being replaced in the summer of 1898 by the first ex-Furness Railway single wheeler, which adopted her name.

Author's Collection

0-6-0 tank *Portishead* . Built by Robert Stephenson & Co. in 1887 and previously used in the construction of the Freshwater, Yarmouth & Newport Railway in the Isle of Wight, where it was named *Longdown*. Purchased by WC&PT in 1898 and sold to the Renishaw Iron Works at Sheffield in 1901 remaining there until the late 1930s.

Author's Collection

These two photographs show *Portishead* working at the Renishaw Iron Works in about 1937. The nameplate has been removed from the right hand side. It was painted in the livery adopted by the WC&PR of crimson lake lined out with vermilion and black, although it is believed that the two single wheelers retained their Furness Railway livery, similar to the Midland Railway's red. *Author's Collection*

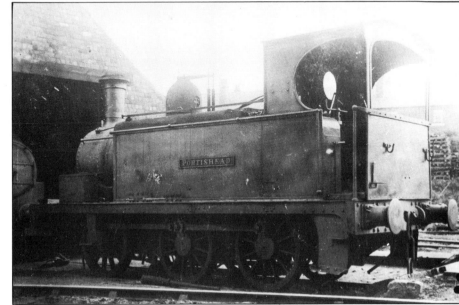

The second *Clevedon* seen here on the Milton Road crossing near Weston-super-Mare in the summer of 1898. Note the crossing gates which were removed about one year later after the line attained light railway status. This locomotive was purchased by the WC&PT from the Furness Railway in early 1898 and delivered to Clevedon after overhaul and the fitting of a new cab by the Avonside Engine Co. of Bristol. A class B2 2-2-2 well tank built by Sharp Stewart in 1857, it became No. 12A on the Furness Railway and worked for some time on the Coniston branch. *L&GRP*

Clevedon on a Clevedon to Weston train near Bristol Road in about 1900. The nameplates were those previously fitted to the Walker Brothers engine and which finally ended up on the little Dübs locomotive in 1906. This *Clevedon* is believed to have been broken up at Clevedon in about 1904.
Author's Collection

The first *Weston* was purchased from the Furness Railway (their number 35) in June 1899. A class B3 2-2-2 well tank built in 1864 by Sharp Stewart, this engine had larger dimensions than those of *Clevedon*, 15″ x 18″ cylinders instead of 14″ x 18″, and a larger boiler. It proved to be more powerful and versatile than *Clevedon*, remaining in use on the line for a longer period until finally sold to a Bristol scrap merchant in 1906. The photograph above shows her with gleaming brasswork at Weston in July 1899 shortly after her arrival on the line, and below near Wick St. Lawrence in 1905. Driver George Hancock appears on the footplate in both these pictures.

Author's Collection

The *General Don* at Weston in 1905, the longest serving locomotive on the WC&PR, purchased in 1901 and eventually broken up at Swindon in 1940 after closure of the line. Built in 1879 by Dübs for the Jersey Railway where it remained until that railway was converted to narrow gauge in 1884. Its history after that date is somewhat obscure and it is believed to have been a contractors engine until its acquisition by the WC&PR. Note cut away cab and absence of vacuum brakes.   *Author's Collection*

On arrival at Clevedon in 1901 it was due to be overhauled and fitted with a new cab and vacuum brakes by the Avonside Engine Co. but in fact did not find its way there until early 1906. Soon after, it was photographed at Wick St. Lawrence in 1906 when nameplates from the single wheeler *Clevedon* had been affixed. One of these is now in the possession of the Bristol Railway Circle, in spite of reports that they were removed during the first World War to help the war effort.

Colonel Stephens Railway Collection

14

Clevedon at Clevedon in October 1937. This locomotive was in regular use until December 1926 when it was involved in a minor accident. One of the coupling rods broke and penetrated the water tank and it was taken out of service and placed at the rear of one of the engine sheds for the next nine years. In late 1935 it was overhauled and repainted mid-green, with black and white lining and chrome yellow lettering, and brought back into service the following year. *R. G. Jarvis*

With a train of original American style coaches at Clevedon in September 1936, about to depart for Weston. Not until 1906 did the company adopt the policy of numbering its locomotives when *Clevedon* was given the number 1.

No. 1 *Clevedon* at the rear of the locomotive shed at Clevedon in 1935 preparatory to overhaul and repainting. This engine had various liveries over the years, originally being painted red, a colour adopted by the company before the first World War. In the early twenties all locomotives, excluding *Hesperus* and No. 5 were repainted a light apple green. Following refurbishment this engine was repainted yet again, in mid-green, as described before.   *S. W. Baker*

No.1 at Clevedon in April 1936.

This photograph taken in the summer of 1937 shows *Clevedon* just arrived from Weston taking on water at Clevedon before proceeding to Portishead. Guard Dan Carey is collecting the tickets. *Clevedon* was the least powerful of the company's fleet and was mainly used for light passenger work.
C. R. L. Coles

To cope with the extra traffic during the summer months of 1903/5/7/8 the company hired from C. D. Phillips of the Emlyn Engineering Works, Newport, two saddle tanks. The one shown here is *Emlyn No. 82*, a Kitson 0-6-0 saddle tank (shown here running as an 0-4-2 at Weston in the summer of 1905) with 14" x 18" inside cylinders and 3' 4" wheels. There was no vacuum brake. Also hired at the same time from the same firm was a Black Hawthorn 0-6-0 saddle tank, *Emlyn No. 96.*   *Author's Collection*

This 2-4-0 tank locomotive was built by Sharp Stewart in 1872 and was originally owned by the LBSCR where it was No. 53, later 497, *Bishopstone* and worked the Hayling Island branch. Sold in 1890 to Cohen of Nottingham from whom it was purchased in 1903 by the WC&PR. Alleged by J. H. P. Capell to have been called *Portishead* it was either sold or broken up at Clevedon in 1906. It was involved in the worst fatal accident in the railway's history when it collided, on 31 August 1903, with a wagonette on the level crossing at Worle, killing two women.   *Author's Collection*

0-6-0 saddle tank No. 3 *Weston*, the second locomotive on the line to carry this name. Built by Manning Wardle in 1881 for J. M. Bury who named it *Resolute*, it was subsequently with various owners until 1894 when it went to the Burry Port & Gwendraeth Valley Railway. In August 1904 it was sold to the Avonside Engine Co. of Bristol who overhauled it in early 1906, fitting an enlarged cab which took in the coal bunker, and at the same time extending the saddle tank. They also painted it red. The WC&PR acquired the engine in early 1906 and the photograph shows her at Weston in June of that year. The brass plate on the side of the cab proclaims 'The Avonside Engine Co. – Rebuilt by – 1906 – Bristol' and was replaced by the oval nameplate from the single wheeler when it was scrapped a few months later. It is shown running as an 0-4-2, the rear coupling rods having been removed to facilitate access on to the GWR connection at Clevedon.   *Author's Collection*

Regarded by the staff as one of the better locomotives owned by the company, No. 3 *Weston*, seen here at Clevedon in 1907, was undoubtedly one of the most powerful and gave good service until withdrawn in early 1938. In latter days *Weston* was virtually worn out and was described as 'being on the jiggle' with many of the parts obviously loose. It exuded large amounts of steam and, when moving, emitted a most audible wheezing sound. Another feature was the unusually high pitched whistle which announced the forthcoming arrival long before it came into view.   *L&GRP*

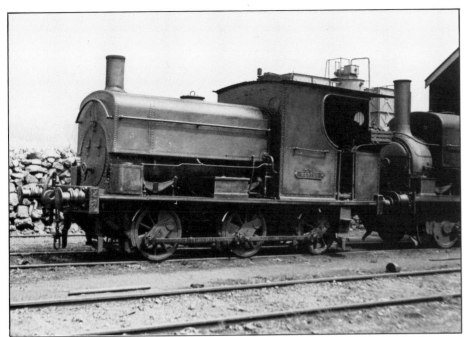

0-6-0 saddle tank *Weston* photographed with No. 5 at Clevedon on 13 July 1935. The oval brass nameplate has been replaced by a cast iron one. *S. W. Baker*

Locomotive No. 2 *Portishead*, the second engine to bear this name. An 0-6-0 saddle tank built by Manning Wardle in 1890, it was purchased in 1907 from Jackson of Stowmarket who was contractor for the Portishead extension. Prior to this the locomotive had several owners, including Logan & Hemingway and Naylor Bros; both were contractors. The latter was responsible for the construction of the Ashbourne & Parsley Hay Light Railway. *Portishead* was used to haul the first train to Portishead on 7 August 1907. The photograph shows *Portishead* with a mixed train at Weston in 1908. Note the fluted chimney which was replaced in 1916 by one of stove pipe design. *J. H. P. Capell*

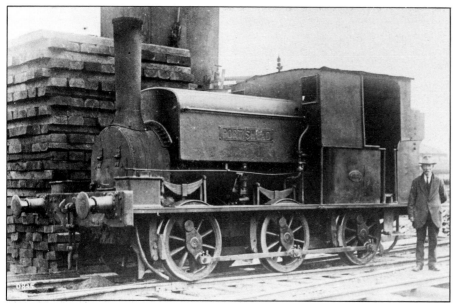

Portishead at the Portishead power station site in 1927, having been sold to William Cowlin of Bristol in 1926 to be used on the construction work. The author remembers seeing the engine derelict in a siding near the site in the early thirties still showing much of its original pale green livery. It was scrapped soon afterwards.

H. G. W. Household

No. 2 *Portishead* at Clevedon in December 1920. Note stove pipe chimney.

E. H. Hazell

A crowd gathers to witness the departure of the first train to Portishead at 8.10 a.m. on 7 August 1907. Seen here headed by 0-6-0 saddle tank *Portishead* crossing the Clevedon Triangle in front of the GWR station. Note the wooden plank being used as a temporary barrier before the installation of crossing gates.   *Author's Collection*

Walton Park was the first new locomotive purchased by the company and was delivered in June 1908. Built by Hudswell Clarke of Leeds to their standard 0-6-0 saddle tank pattern. The most powerful engine to run on the line and also the heaviest. It was for the latter reason that it was transferred to another of the Stephens' lines, the Plymouth, Devonport & South Western Junction Railway on 15 March 1912. It was later reported to have worked on the Shropshire & Montgomeryshire Railway before being transferred to the East Kent Railway in 1917, and where this photograph was taken in the early thirties. Remaining there until 1940 it changed hands two more times and was eventually scrapped in 1957.   *R. G. Jarvis*

Walton Park at Clevedon in 1908, shortly after arrival in new Midland red livery
Colonel Stephens Railway Collection

2-4-0 side tank *Hesperus* built by Sharp Stewart in 1875 for the Watlington & Princes Risborough Railway, a line that was absorbed by the GWR in 1883. On the latter it was numbered 1384 and seems to have had a varied career, working the first trains on the Lambourn Valley Railway. In 1899 it emerged from a rebuild at Swindon with a distinctive GWR appearance and was then used for a short period on the Wrington Vale Light Railway and then on the Culm Valley branch. Here No. 1384 is seen at Portishead in April 1911 shortly after arrival on the WC&PR, and where it ran in this condition for some time before receiving the name *Hesperus*.   *Author's Collection*

No. 4 *Hesperus* at Clevedon in 1935 lined up with Nos. 3 and 1.   *R. G. Jarvis*

After the incident at Wick St. Lawrence in 1934 when a small wooden bridge on the approach to the jetty collapsed under the weight of *Hesperus* the locomotive was little used and after spending some time at the rear of the carriage sheds was removed in June 1937 to a siding and broken up. Mr W. E. Hayward of Weston-super-Mare managed to secure one of the nameplates for half-a-crown and this now forms part of the Light Railway exhibit at the Weston Museum. The other plate was unfortunately broken whilst being removed.

Northiam was hired from the Kent & East Sussex Railway from about 1917 to 1921; precise dates are unknown but it was definitely photographed by Edwin Hazell at Clevedon in December 1920. Well known for its appearance in the Will Hay film 'Oh Mr Porter' *Northiam* was a 2-4-0 side tank with outside cylinders built by Hawthorn Leslie in 1899. Eventually scrapped in 1941 and seen here on the K&ESR in about 1937.
Author's Collection

The second new engine purchased by the WC&PR was No. 5, delivered to Clevedon on 18 April 1919. A Manning Wardle 0-6-0 saddle tank, it was moderately powerful and extensively used up to the end. Painted dark green when first delivered it soon became very grimy and little of the original livery remained during the later years. It is here at Clevedon on 13 July 1935 in a 'line-up' with Nos. 3 and 4. Note the disc wheels which were specifically ordered by Colonel Stephens. Its fate after the line's closure in 1940 is unknown.   *S. W. Baker*

No. 5 with a mixed train from Portishead approaching Parnell Road crossing at Clevedon in September 1937. The gas works siding is off to the right.

No. 2 *Portishead*, the third locomotive to carry this name and one of the famous Brighton Terriers, at Clevedon on 9 May 1938. Formerly No. 43 *Gipsyhill* on the LBSCR it was bought from the Southern Railway in December 1925 and arrived at Clevedon still bearing traces of LBSCR livery. This engine was quite powerful and gave stalwart service, especially in hauling large loads of stone from the Black Rock Quarries. It was in regular use on the line up to the end, and after being taken over by the GWR in 1940 was in continual use by them until 1950.

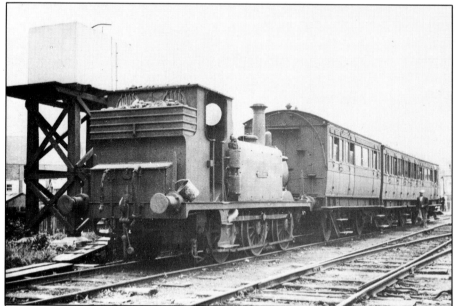

A Weston train at Clevedon on Whitsun Bank Holiday Monday, 6 June 1938, headed by No. 2 *Portishead*. Up until this time the locomotive had always faced in the other direction but for some reason was turned at Portishead, probably to even out wear on the wheel flanges.

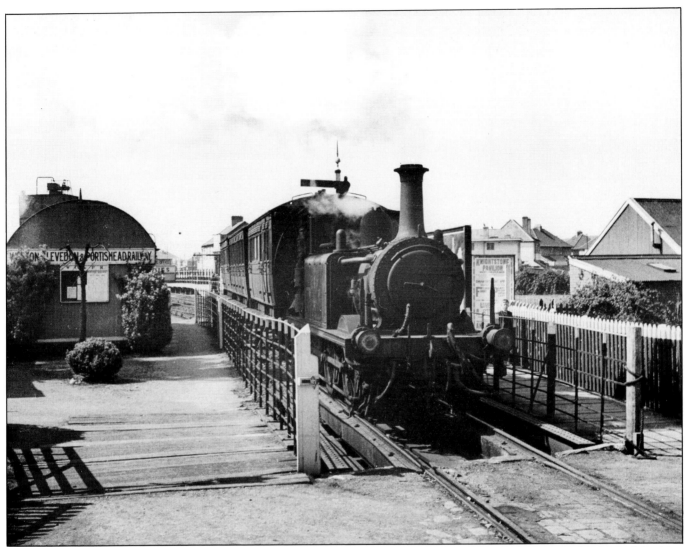

By 1936 the WC&PR was having problems with its motive power. No. 1 was only suitable for light duties, No. 2 was being overhauled, No. 3 was on its last legs and No. 4 was about to be scrapped, leaving only No. 5 for use. After considering various alternatives, such as hiring a locomotive from the GWR, it was decided to purchase another engine. Another Stroudley Terrier was acquired from the Southern Railway; No. 2653, formerly LBSCR No. 53 *Ashtead*. It arrived at Clevedon on 12 February 1937 and was immediately placed at the rear of the carriage shed. Howard Carey recalls being taken by his father, Dan Carey (a guard on the line at the time), to see this locomotive the following day and when the tarpaulin was drawn back the engine still displayed its Southern livery. Soon afterwards it was painted in its new colours of mid green and black with white linings and became No. 4. The company's logo was painted in chrome yellow letters using a large stencil kept in the carpenters' shop. This stencil was also used for painting the white letters on the three original coaches and the logo on No. 1. No. 4 is here on a train for Portishead leaving Clevedon on Easter Bank Holiday Monday, 18 April 1938. The carriages are the ex-LSWR close coupled set known as the triplet.

No. 4 at Clevedon in October 1937. This engine was used for hauling the last public trains on 18 May 1940 and was taken into stock by the GWR following closure of the line. It was eventually scrapped in 1948.

R. G. Jarvis

Driver Tom Gatford seen here on the footplate of Terrier No. 4 at Clevedon in September 1937. Mr Gatford was the senior driver on the WC&PR and came to Clevedon in 1936 from the Shropshire & Montgomeryshire Railway, another of Colonel Stephens' lines. He remained with the company until the line closed in 1940. He was a former Regimental Sergeant Major, hence the shine on his boots.

The WC&PR was the first of the Colonel Stephens' lines to operate a petrol driven railcar. In 1921 the Drewry Car Co. Ltd. constructed a railcar to Colonel Stephens' specifications and it was delivered to Clevedon in October of that year. Powered by a water cooled four cylinder Baguley engine which developed 25–35 h.p., it was equipped with a three speed gear box operating in forward and reverse directions. It had a maximum speed of about 25 m.p.h. and a seating capacity of 30. Running costs were low and its consequent economy led to the company becoming profitable for a short time. This mode of transport proved very popular and a matching trailer was ordered from the same supplier, being delivered in March 1923. The trailer seated 24 passengers and originally protection from inclement weather was provided by canvas curtains but these were subsequently replaced by drop windows. This view is of the railcar at Clevedon in September 1937 coupled to a small open wagon built by Cranes (Dereham) Ltd. After closure the railcar was transported on a well wagon to Swindon where it was scrapped.

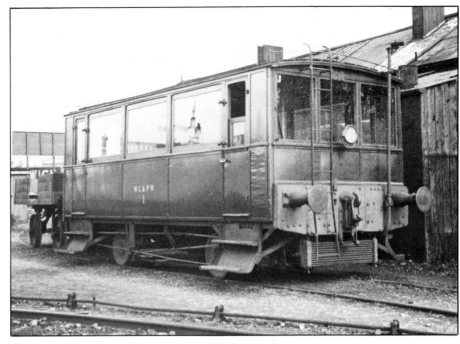

A maker's photograph of the railcar trailer taken prior to delivery. *Author's Collection*

The small Drewry railcar with Cranes open wagon approaching Clevedon from Weston in 1938. This wagon was used mainly for the delivery and collection of milk churns at various points between Clevedon and Weston. The railcar was fitted with a most unusual whistle which was operated from the engine's exhaust and produced an intermittent warbling sound.

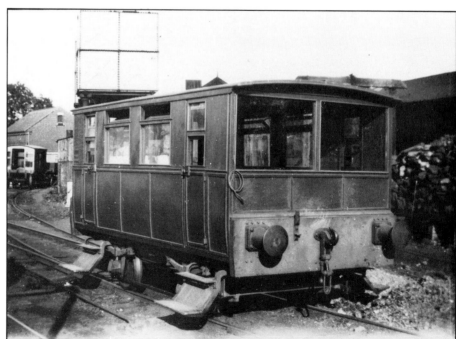

The Drewry trailer, with modified windows, at Clevedon in August 1936.

INTERNAL COMBUSTION
RAILWAY MOTOR CARS, INSPECTION CARS AND LOCOMOTIVES

50 H.P. FOUR WHEEL COMPOSITE COACH FOR BRANCH LINE SERVICES.

The most economical units for branch line and intermittent services, particularly in cases where road motor competition has to be contended with. Coaches can be supplied mounted on four wheels or double bogies, and fitted with bodies to suit individual requirements.

DREWRY WILL REDUCE YOUR OPERATING COSTS

THE DREWRY CAR COMPANY LTD.
13 SOUTH PLACE   LONDON, E.C.2

Telegrams: " Inneal, London."
Telephone: London Wall 4254.

WORKS:
BURTON
ON-TRENT

The second petrol driven railcar was featured in this Drewry Car Co's advertisement, which appeared in the *Locomotive Magazine* on 15 May 1929. Built in 1928 for the Southern Railway it was powered by a 50 h.p. engine, replaced in about 1930 with a 64 h.p. engine. It had a seating capacity of 22 and a large luggage compartment. Purchased by the company in 1934 it was mainly used on the Weston-super-Mare section. It retained on the WC&PR not only its number 5 but also its Southern livery, the words 'Southern Railway' being replaced by the letters 'W.C. & P.'. It was removed to Swindon along with the other rolling stock in August 1940 and the body eventually ended up as a pavilion at a Swindon girls' school.

Author's Collection

Interior of large railcar. The seating was upholstered in red and black patterned moquette and the rear of the seats could be moved enabling the passengers to face the direction of travel. Separate drivers' compartments were situated at each end with a large luggage compartment adjacent to the passengers' seating area, accessible through double doors. Additional seating capacity was sometimes provided by attaching the small Drewry trailer at the rear.

The large Drewry railcar at Clevedon in October 1937 waiting to depart for Weston. This vehicle had a 20 feet wheelbase, weighed 10 tons 17 cwt and was of standard railway carriage height, as opposed to the smaller vehicle acquired some thirteen years previously. Transmission was through a three speed gearbox operating in both directions and there were electric head-lamps fitted at each end. *R. G. Jarvis*

Large Drewry railcar approaching Mud Lane bound for Weston in September 1937. Mud Lane, appropriately named, was a stopping point halfway between Ham Lane and Wick St. Lawrence used for the collection and return of milk churns belonging to local dairy farmers.

Abbreviations:

BH	Black Hawthorn & Co. Ltd.
DC	Drewry Car Co. Ltd.
HC	Hudswell, Clarke & Co. Ltd.
HL	R. & W. Hawthorn, Leslie & Co. Ltd.
K&ESR	Kent & East Sussex Railway
LBSCR	London Brighton & South Coast Railway
MH	Muir Hill Engineering Ltd.
MW	Manning, Wardle & Co. Ltd.
RS	Robert Stephenson & Co.
SS	Sharp Stewart & Co. Ltd.
WkB	Walker Bros (Wigan) Ltd.
W&PRR	Watlington & Princes Risborough Railway

LOCOMOTIVES

No:	Name:	Type:	Maker	No.	Built	Bought	Original owner	Disposed
	Harold	0-6-0ST	Kitson	1829	1872	(1897)	Hired	1898
	Clevedon	0-6-0T	WkB			1897		1898
	Clevedon	2-2-2WT	SS	1017	1857	1898	Furness Railway 12A	c1904
	Weston	2-2-2WT	SS	1707	1866	1899	Furness Railway 35	1906
	Portishead	0-6-0T	RS	2383	1887	1898		1901
1	Clevedon	2-4-0T	Dübs	1222	1879	1901	Jersey Railway	1940
	Emlyn No 82	0-6-0ST	Kitson			(1903)	Hired	1907
	–	2-4-0T	SS	2242	1872	1903	LBSCR 53, later 497	1906
	Emlyn No 96	0-6-0ST	BH			(1905)	Hired	1905
3	Weston	0-6-0ST	MW	731	1881	1906	J. M. Smith	1940
2	Portishead	0-6-0ST	MW	1134	1890	1907	Logan & Hemingway	1926
(4)	Walton Park	0-6-0ST	HC	823	1908	1908	New	1912
4	Hesperus	2-4-0T	SS	2578	1876	1911	W&PRR (GWR 1384)	1937
2	Northiam	2-4-0T	HL	2420	1899	(1917)	On loan from K&ESR	1921
5	–	0-6-0ST	MW	1970	1919	1919	New	1940
2	Portishead	0-6-0T	LBSCR		1877	1925	LBSCR 43	1940
4	–	0-6-0T	LBSCR		1875	1937	LBSCR 53	1940
	Tractor	2-2wPM	MH		1921		New	1926
	Tractor	4wPM	MH	A137	1926	1926	New	1940
	Railcar		DC	1252	1921	1921	New	1940
	Railcar		DC	1650	1928	1934	Southern Railway	1940

The first rail tractor to be used, mainly for shunting on the Yeo jetty at Wick St. Lawrence. Built by Muir-Hill Service Equipment Ltd. of Manchester, and purchased by the company in 1921. This vehicle was basically a Fordson tractor converted by fitting special flanged dished rear wheels 40 inches in diameter mounted direct on the tractor live axle shaft and a special front axle fitted with flanged wheels 24 inches in diameter. It weighed 46 cwt and had a haulage capacity of 60 tons. This tractor was damaged beyond repair when it jumped the track while being towed back to Clevedon. Photographed here at Clevedon in 1921 shortly after arrival on the line.   *E. H. Hazell*

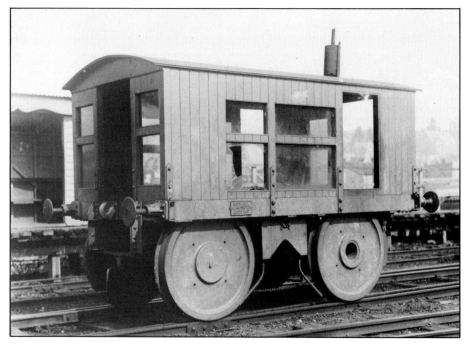

After the demise of tractor number 1 a further vehicle was purchased from the same company in 1926. Once again, basically a Fordson tractor driven by a four cylinder water cooled engine but with four cast flanged wheels of 40 inches diameter. It weighed four tons, had a hauling capacity of 75 tons and was also fitted with sandboxes, spring buffers and drawhooks. It arrived as a chassis and power unit only and had its glass panelled cab fitted in the carpenter's shop at Clevedon. Seen here at Clevedon, April 1928.   *H. G. W. Household*

The first six carriages acquired by the WC&PT were always referred to as cars and were of a distinct American style. Originally built for the Argentine Republic Railway by the Lancaster Railway Carriage & Wagon Co. Ltd. they were obtained cheaply after the original contract fell through. However, they were ordered in sufficient time to allow the makers to provide cast iron axle box covers inscribed 'Weston and Clevedon Tramways'. These cars were delivered in crates in 'kit' form and assembled at Clevedon some time before the line was officially opened. They had centre corridors, straight sides and clerestorey roofs. The bodies were made entirely of mahogany in sections for easy shipping. The end platforms had wrought ironwork and gates at the ends to enable the conductor to pass from one car to another. Steps were also provided for access at stations without elevated platforms; these steps were removed when the cars were taken up to Swindon after closure. Car 2 is shown at Swindon on 21 August 1940 with the steps removed. The interior view shows the layout of the seating. The last three coaches were of this design but some of the other three, which were sold or scrapped in 1935, had tramway type transverse seating with seat backs hinged to allow the passenger to face either direction.

Seats in the first class section were provided with arm rests and upholstered in black leather. Automatic vacuum braking was fitted throughout in addition to the chain brake which was operated by a wheel on each platform. Being of bogie type they gave a very smooth ride. However, if the end doors were left open smoke from the engine sometimes passed down the length of the car to the discomfort of the passengers. Little used during the twenties and early thirties these cars were placed at the rear of the carriage sheds and on the long dump siding at Clevedon. In 1935 two of the cars were sold, a third was acquired by fitter Hill and used as a garden shed. The remaining three were refurbished and painted dark green with white lettering, and brought back into service in 1936 numbered 1, 2 and 4. These cars had the distinction of being the first vehicles in Great Britain to be illuminated by acetylene gas, a system devised by the Traffic Manager, Mr

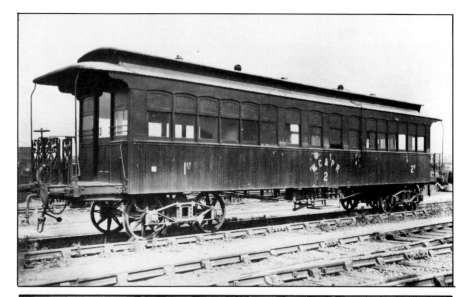

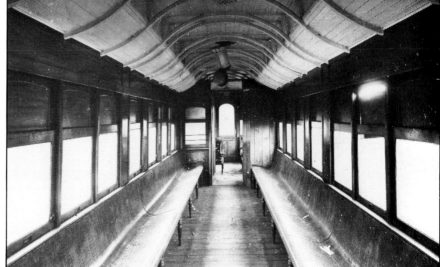

E. R. Wintour, which replaced the initial mineral oil lamps. These cars were originally painted red and traces of this colour were still visible well into the early thirties. After removal to Swindon one was used as a hut and the two others were acquired by a school in Melksham and used as dormitories. *Official GWR Photograph*

The interior of one of the original American type cars. Note the black leather upholstered seats in the first class section.

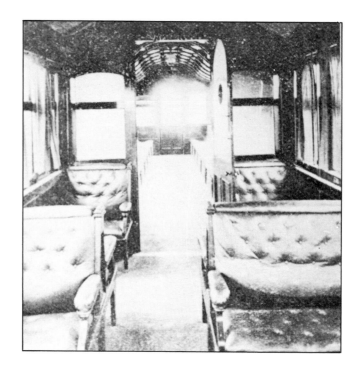

The remains of a seventh coach bought in 1901 from the Great Central Railway. It was an open vehicle and alleged to have been used during the summer months as a 'smoking' car. It was numbered 7 but renumbered 13 in the wagon stock in 1913 and left in the former passing loop at Wick St. Lawrence where it was photographed in September 1937. What is shown is all that remains of the bottom half of this coach. It was known to the staff as the 'old chara-banc'. The axle boxes were inscribed 'Gorton N 21'.

This brass oval plate was carried by this coach and its original position can be clearly seen in the photograph of the remains to the right of the WC&PR cast iron plate.

After the extension to Portishead was opened on 7 August 1907 the company purchased from the Metropolitan Railway seven four wheeled coaches which had become redundant after electrification. They were originally built by Craven's Carriage & Wagon Co. Ltd of Sheffield in 1870 and entered sevice on the WC&PR on 2 September 1907. Consisting of three close coupled pairs and one single, they were numbered 8 and 13, 9 and 10, 11 and 12, and lastly the single coach numbered 7. No. 7 is shown here at Swindon on 21 August 1940. Note the absence of steps. No. 7 was all one class and fitted with longitudinal wooden seats. The other coaches were first and second class and the seats were upholstered in red moquette in the first class section and plain wood in the second. All compartments were linked by doors and side corridors. They were provided with Pintsch's patent gas lighting and had hand brakes in addition to vacuum brakes. Originally painted Midland red, subsequent livery was dark brown with black lining and yellow lettering. The coach ends were painted red. No. 7 was rescued from Shrivenham where it was being used as a shop and should now have been completely restored at the Ruislip Transport Museum.

Official GWR Photograph

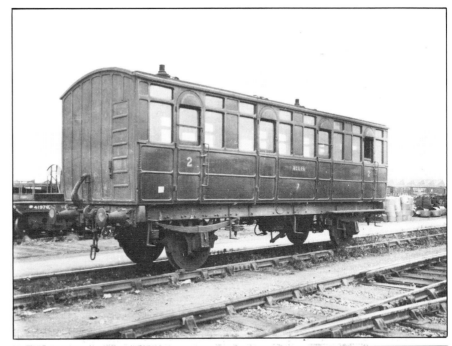

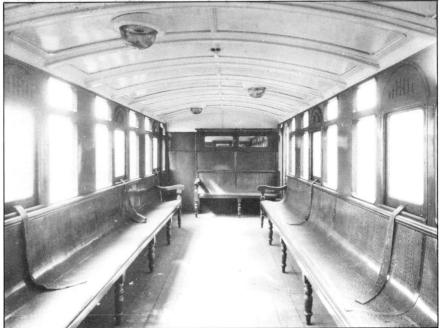

Close coupled ex-Metropolitan Railway coaches Nos. 8 and 13 at Clevedon on 6 June 1938.

Ex-Great Eastern Railway four wheeled brake van on the dump siding at Clevedon on 25 June 1938. The precise date of acquisition of the vehicle is unknown but believed to be 1911. Numbered 14 by the WC&PR it was in use mainly for the conveyance of milk churns and other goods until it was derailed at Worle Town on 13 July 1927. It was then removed to Clevedon and not used again. No.14 was scrapped on site in 1940 after closure. *H. C. Casserley*

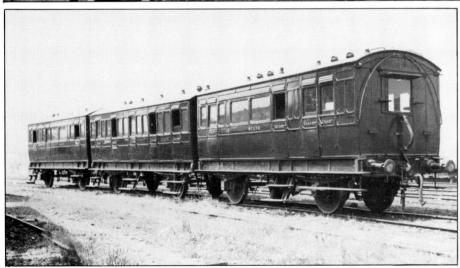

In 1924 the WC&PR purchased from the Southern Railway three more four wheeled coaches of LSWR origin. They operated as a close coupled set and were referred to as the 'triplet' although occassionally the set would be run with the centre coach omitted. Numbered 15, 16 and 17, no. 15 contained a guard's brake compartment, a central saloon for second class passengers and a first class compartment. No. 16 had five second class compartments while no. 17, which was also second class, had a compartment at each end giving access to a central saloon which had seating along the sides. Second class seats were upholstered in black and red moquette and the first class seats in blue cloth. Electric light was provided by a dynamo on no. 15 and the set had steam heating. These coaches were probably in use during the latter years more than any other on the line and provided a very comfortable ride. The upper photograph shows the triplet arriving at Clevedon from Weston behind No. 4 on Easter Bank Holiday Monday 18 April 1938. The lower one shows the coaches at Clevedon on 13 July 1935.   *Lower: S. W. Baker*

Coach 18. It is not certain when this coach was purchased but it was acquired to replace the ex-Great Eastern Railway four wheeled brake van after it was derailed at Worle Town in 1927. Known as the 'Taff Vale Coach' after its origin before being taken over by the GWR who in turn sold it to the WC&PR. A four wheel vehicle with two second class compartments, a large luggage section and a guard's compartment with side lookouts. It was painted dark green with white lettering and was used during off-peak periods, mainly in the winter months. At Clevedon in September 1937.

Coach 18 as part of a mixed train hauled by No. 4 bound for Portishead crossing the Clevedon to Portishead road near Walton Park in December 1937.

The rolling stock was formed into two trains on the morning of Sunday 21 August 1940 and towed at a maximum speed of 10 m.p.h. to Swindon, via Badminton. All carriage steps were removed prior to the journey to prevent the fouling of station platforms en-route. The locomotives (except Nos. 3 and 5) were taken up to Swindon from Bristol at different times.   *Official GWR Photograph*

CARRIAGE STOCK

Nos:	Builder:	Built:	Bought:	Origin:	Disposal:
1-6	Lancaster Carriage & Wagon Co.	1897	1897	New	1935-40
7	(later wagon 13) Great Central Railway?	?	1901	Great Central Railway	1940
7-13	Cravens	1870	1907	Metropolitan Railway	1940
14	?	?	c1911	Great Eastern Railway	1940
15-17	?	?	1924	London & South Western Railway	1940
18	?	?	c1927	Taff Vale Railway	1940

A line-up of some of the stock at Swindon on 21 August 1940. These were the only wagons not condemned and broken up at Clevedon. *Official GWR Photograph*

WAGON STOCK

Vehicle No.	Description	Origin
1	Not known	Not known
2	5 plank open wagon	Midland Railway
3	3 plank open wagon	Midland Railway
4	5 plank open wagon	Midland Railway
5 to 12 inclusive	5 plank open wagon	Midland Railway
13	Open passenger vehicle	Great Central Railway
14	3 plank open wagon (7' wheel base)	Midland Railway
15	3 plank open wagon	Midland Railway
16	5 plank open wagon	Midland Railway
17	Machinery wagon	Midland Railway
18	3 plank open wagon	Midland Railway
19	3 plank open wagon (7' wheel base)	Midland Railway
20	3 plank open wagon	Midland Railway
21	5 plank open wagon	Midland Railway
22	3 plank open wagon	Midland Railway
23	3 plank open wagon	Midland Railway
24	5 plank open wagon	Midland Railway
25	5 plank open wagon	Midland Railway
26	7 plank open wagon	Midland Railway
27	7 plank open wagon	Midland Railway
	Covered box van	Great Eastern Railway
	Brake van	Midland Railway

The wagon stock at closure consisted of the following, which had been acquired over the years. All these vehicles were painted light grey with white lettering and numbers. Finally there were four inspection trolleys including one which was petrol driven. The author does not recall ever having seen the latter and it is assumed that it did not last long. The others remained at Clevedon after closure and were left to rot.

Ashcombe Road, Weston-super-Mare terminus, in the summer of 1898. The fence in the foreground masks the path of the proposed tramway extension along the public highway to the Boulevard, which was never completed. The house on the right was the residence of Mr E. R. Wintour, the traffic manager. The name of the company – Weston, Clevedon & Portishead Tramways – was inscribed on the ground floor bay windows. This building is now a chemist's shop and a florist occupies the land behind the fencing. *W. Vaughan-Jenkins*

OMNIBUS TIME TABLE.

The Pier and Ashcombe Road or Shaftesbury.

		a.m	a.m	a.m	a.m	a.m	p.m	p.m	p.m	p.m	p.m	p.m	p.m	p.m	p.m	
The Pier	dep.		10 17	11	0	11 47	12 20	2 32	3 15	4 54	32 5	10 6	15 7	18		
Knightstone			10 20	11	3	11 50	12 25	2 36	3 18	4 84	35 5	13 6	18 7	21		
Shaftesbury	arr.		11	8					3 24	3 54		5 18	6	24		
*Boulevard (Bryant's)	dep		10 26			11 56	12 28	2 41			4 40			7	26		
Ashcombe Road	arr.		10 30			12	0	12 32	2 45			4 45			7	30
Ashcombe Road	dep.		10 35			12	5		2 50			4 50			7	35
*Boulevard (Bryant's)	dep		10 38			12	8		2 53			4 53			7	38
Shaftesbury	dep.	10	0			11 20		2 15		3 30	4 15		6	0 6	30	7 44
Knightstone		10	5	10 45	11 25	12 15	2 20	3	0	3 35	4 20	5	0 6	5 6	35	
The Pier	arr.	10	8	10 48	11 28	12 18	2 24	3	4	3 38	4 24	5	3 6	8 6	38	

The Sanatorium and Ashcombe Road.

		a.m	a.m	a.m	a.m	p.m	p.m	p.m	p.m	p.m	p.m	p.m	
Sanatorium	dep.		10 15	11	0	11 45	12 30	2 30	3 15	4	0 4	30 5	15 6	30 7	15
*Regent St. (Ashford's)			10 22	11	7	11 52	12 37	2 37	3 22	4	7 4	37 5	22 6	37 7	22
*Boulevard (Bryant's)			10 26	11 12	11 56	12 42	2 41	3 26	4	12 4	41 5	26 6	41 7	26	
Ashcombe Road	arr.		10 30			12	0	12 45	2 45			4 45			7	30
Ashcombe Road	dep.		10 35			12	5		2 50			4 50			7	35
*Boulevard (Bryant's)		10	0	10 38	11 20	12	8	2	15	2 53	3 45	4	15 4	54 5	38 7	38
*Regent St. (Ashford's)		10	4	10 42	11 24	12 12	2	18	2 57	3 48	4	18 4	57 6	18 6	48 7	42
Sanatorium	arr.	10	10	10 50	11 30	12 20	2	25	3	5 3	54 4	25 5	5 6	25 6	56

*Waiting Rooms. **Refreshments always ready at ASHFORD'S Dining Rooms.

This Time Table is printed by Huntley Bros., Royal Arcades, Weston-s-Mare. Estimates given

Nov. & Dec.]   **TIME TABLE.**   [1898.

DOWN

		a.m	a.m	a.m	p.m	p.m	p.m	p.m		p.m	p.m	p.m	p.m	p.m	p.m	p.m
Clevedon	dep...	8	15	10	0	11 30	2	15	4	15	*Saturdays only*	9	0	9	0		2	15 5	0 8	15
Colehouse Lane	,,	8	18	10	3	11 33	2	18	4	18		9	3	9	3		2	18 5	3 8	18
Kingston Road	,,	8	22	10	7	11 37	2	22	4	22		9	7	9	7		2	22 5	7 8	22
Ham Lane	,,	8	26	10 11	11 41	2	26	4	26		9	11	9	11		2	26 5	11 8	26
Wick St. Lawrence	,,	8	30	10 15	11 45	2	30	4	30		9	16	9	16		2	30 5	16 8	30
Ebdon Lane	,,	8	33	10 18	11 48	2	33	4	33		9	20	9	20		2	33 5	20 8	33
Worle	,,	8	38	10 23	11 53	2	38	4	38		9	25	9	25		2	38 5	25 8	38
Milton Road	,,	8	42	10 28	11 58	2	42	4	42		9	30	9	30		2	42 5	30 8	43
Weston-s-Mare	arr.	8	46	10 32	12	2	2	46	4	46		9	35	9	35		2	46 5	33 8	48

UP

		a.m	a.m	a.m	p.m	p.m	p.m		p.m	p.m	p.m	p.m	p.m	p.m	p.m
Weston-s-Mare	dep...	9	0	10 45	12 15	3	0	5	0	7	45	*10 0*	*Saturdays only*	3	0 5	45 9	0
Milton Road	,,	9	3	10 48	12 18	3	3	5	3	7	49	*10 4*		3	3 5	48 9	4
Worle	,,	9	8	10 53	12 23	3	8	5	8	7	55	*10 10*		3	8 5	54 9	10
Ebdon Lane	,,	9	13	10 57	12 28	3	13	5	13	8	0	*10 15*		3	13 5	59 9	15
Wick St. Lawrence	,,	9	17	11	1	12 32	3	17	5	17	8	4	*10 19*		3	17 6	3 9	19
Ham Lane	,,	9	21	11	5	12 36	3	21	5	21	8	10	*10 23*		3	21 6	7 9	23
Kingston Road	,,	9	26	11 10	12 41	3	26	5	26	8	14	*10 28*		3	26 6	12 9	28
Colehouse Lane	,,	9	30	11 13	12 45	3	30	5	30	8	17	*10 32*		3	30 6	16 9	32
Clevedon	arr.	9	34	11 16	12 48	3	34	5	34	8	21	*10 36*		3	34 6	20 9	36

The Trams will not run on Christmas Day.

The Company's Omnibusses meet all Trains at Weston. See other side for times.

E. R. WINTOUR, Traffic Manager.

Huntley Bros., Printers and Advertisement Contractors, Royal Arcades, Weston-s-Mare.

In the early days a horse drawn omnibus service was provided between Ashcombe Road terminus and the old pier via the Boulevard, run by the company. This photograph shows the omnibus at Ashcombe Road in about 1900.

Colonel Stephens Railway Collection

Ashcombe Road terminus in 1908. Note the low wooden platform which remained in situ until 1919 when elevated platforms were constructed at Weston and Clevedon. The track between these two points was laid with flat bottomed rails 30 feet long and weighing 56 lbs per yard, secured to sleepers of half round section. The latter had not properly been treated and soon after the line was opened they had to be renewed throughout. This type of sleeper is to be seen in the photograph of the *Harold* at the beginning of this album. The shunting neck and buffer stops were removed shortly after this photograph was taken. At the same time a loop and siding were provided at the opposite end of the platform, locked with Annett's key and the staff for the section.

Author's Collection

Station buildings at Weston-super-Mare in April 1921. The accomodation consisted of ticket office, waiting room and toilets.

E. H. Hazell

View of Weston terminus showing track, platform and buildings in September 1941, after closure but before the track etc., was lifted.

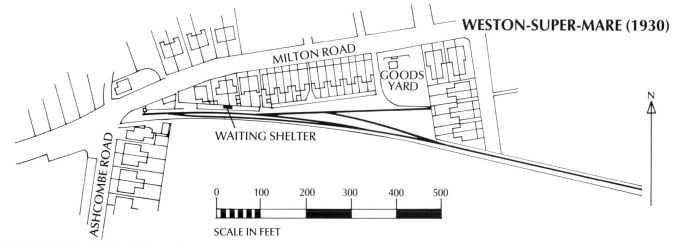

N

0 100 200 300 400 500

SCALE IN FEET

Milton Road, sited at a distance of 1·06 miles from Ashcombe Road terminus, was a halt with an asbestos covered shelter and a siding of approximately 130 yards in length, constructed, oddly enough, with 40 lbs rails. Originally gates were provided at this crossing but were removed in 1899 when the tramway became a light railway. It was then necessary to provide white painted cattle grids and these became standard at all crossings without gates. The only crossing between Weston and Clevedon to have gates was at High Street, Worle, as this crossed what was originally the main road to and from Bristol. *Alan Ball*

Locking Road crossing looking westwards towards Weston. Ths photograph was taken in 1930 before ribbon development along this road obscured views of the open countryside. *R. K. Cope*

47

Locking Road crossing looking east towards Clevedon in 1930. This halt was, in fact, called 'Bristol Road'; the actual Bristol Road crossing was located several hundred yards further along the line towards Worle Town station and was also crossed diagonally. In 1938 both these crossings were provided with traffic lights activated by the trains passing over treadles. The green lights were normally favourable to the road but changed to red on the approach of the train and changed back to green after the expiration of a period pre-set to allow the train to clear the level crossing.   *R. K. Cope*

The next station along the line was Worle Town, sited 1·83 miles from Weston. Originally called Worle, then in 1913 renamed Worle Moor Lane it finally became Worle Town in 1917. On the south side of the main line and to the west of Station Road there was a loop with a shunting neck, and a siding which passed back over Station Road and into the Gas Works. After the latter closed in about 1920 this siding was removed and the layout altered to provide a longer siding and goods yard. The station building, seen here in 1921, comprised booking office and waiting room. In the early years this station was permanently manned. Not shown is the original low wooden platform similar to that at Ashcombe Road which had been removed some years earlier.   *E. H. Hazell*

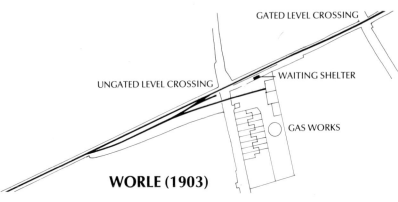

WORLE (1903)

GATED LEVEL CROSSING

UNGATED LEVEL CROSSING

WAITING SHELTER

GAS WORKS

Worle Town loop and siding looking towards Clevedon in September 1941 after the line closed and before the track was removed.

Ebdon Lane halt, 3·09 miles from Weston, was provided with a wooden shelter made by Jennings of Bristol, manufacturers of portable buildings who supplied and erected similar buildings at many of the line's halts and stations. In the nineteen thirties these buildings, including those at Clevedon, were all painted yellow with black plinths and red roofs. This photograph was taken in December 1938 looking towards Clevedon. The halt also had a milk platform which was removed in the early thirties.

At 3·8 miles from Weston, Wick St. Lawrence was regarded as the halfway point
between Clevedon and Weston, and was
the location of a passing loop. These two
photographs, taken in 1910 and December
1938 respectively, show this loop, which
also had shunting necks at each end of the
running side. The passing loop ceased to be
used for this purpose prior to World War I
and the northern side was then used as a
siding together with its shunting neck. Se-
maphore signals were placed at each end of
the loop, as seen in the upper and earlier
photograph, but these were subsequently
removed. The station building was divided
internally in two with a waiting room on the
left and a 'booking hall' on the right, although in fact the latter was used as a store.
Author's Collection

The passing loop at Wick St. Lawrence looking towards Weston in December 1938, the
northern side of the loop and the shunting
neck being used as sidings.

The jetty on the River Yeo in 1921. Access
was by a spur of five chains radius from the
north side of the main line, with a passing
loop. The jetty was 190 feet long and in turn
connected to a landing stage of 80 feet
length. The two consisted of concrete platforms supported by a concrete and wooden
structure. There were storage sheds, a pile
driver and tanks to provide water for the
steam crane.   *E. H. Hazell*

The barge *Edith* unloading steam coal for use on the line at the jetty at Wick St. Lawrence on the morning of 21 September 1937. Four wagons at a time were pushed onto the jetty by the Muir-Hill tractor and when full were pulled back into one side of the loop to make up an eight wagon train for onward transmission to Clevedon. The original steam crane was removed to the shunting neck at the end of the loop at Wick St. Lawrence station in 1931 as it was decided that it was more efficient to use the barges' derricks, as depicted in this photograph.

A further scene at the jetty on 21 September 1937. Four wagons are already on the landing stage receiving coal from the *Edith* while four empties wait in the loop to take their place when filled and moved back to the other side of the loop.

The following day No. 4 pushes the eight loaded wagons back to Clevedon. Photographed here near Kingston Road with guard Jack Riddick riding 'shotgun' on the front wagon.

Looking across the bridge over the River Yeo towards Clevedon in September 1937. The bridge was 240 feet in length and was the last structure to be removed in 1943. All that remains today are the metal supporting columns, which have settled considerably into the mud of the river bed.

Erected at a point where the line crossed an aptly named track leading to local farms, Mud Lane platform was primarily used for milk churn traffic. It was situated approximately halfway between Wick St. Lawrence and Ham Lane. Looking towards Weston in May 1938, the water tanks on the spur to the jetty can be seen in the middle distance.

Ham Lane station was 4·93 miles from Weston and mainly served the local farming community, being provided with a milk platform consisting of the base of an old wagon. September 1937, looking towards Clevedon.

The notice on the side of the building proclaims 'WC&PR – Ham Lane Goods Station – Traffic received from and for all parts'. There was a siding, which held six wagons, and catch points. The only inward traffic was coal but on one occasion turf from the nearby saltings was removed to the Isle of Wight for use on a bowling green, and forty wagons were needed. December 1938, looking towards Weston.

No. 4 on the 10.55 a.m. train to Weston
from Clevedon at Ham Lane on Whitsun
Bank Holiday Monday, 6 June 1938.

Two miles dead straight. Looking towards Clevedon near Broadstone whose halt's shelter can be seen top centre. From time to time the company kept the weeds between the tracks clear by spreading tar from a specially adapted tank wagon and the effects can be clearly seen in this photograph taken in September 1937.

Broadstone halt. Along with Bristol Road this was not opened until 1918 and hence does not appear in timetables before that date. Sufficient land was acquired by the company to install a siding but this was never carried out. Situated 5·25 from Weston, this halt merely had a sentry box type shelter which is shown here in this 1932 photograph with No. 2 *Portishead* on a Clevedon to Weston train. Guard Jack Riddick is riding on the carriage step.

Kingston Road halt was 5·95 miles from Weston and also largely served local farmers. There was a milk platform here until the early thirties but it was subsequently removed. A platelayers hut was sited some 50 yards further towards Weston on the south side of the track. Looking towards Clevedon, December 1937.

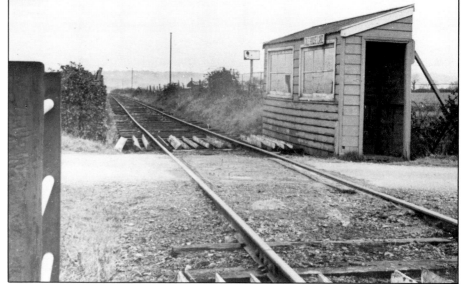

Colehouse Lane, 6·8 miles from Weston, once again served the rural community. This photograph, taken in December 1937 looking towards Clevedon, shows the long narrow shelter. In early 1939 when the BBC constructed their Clevedon transmitter in the adjoining field it was necessary to remove this shelter and erect a new one on the opposite side of the line to make way for access to the transmitter.

Colehouse Lane in March 1939, showing the halt's new shelter relocated on the north side of the line and work in progress to form access to the BBC's new Clevedon transmitter. Note the hand trolley in the foreground.

Taken at the same time as the upper photograph but from some distance further up the line looking towards Clevedon and showing the new transmitter and mast on the right.

Clevedon, the headquarters of the line and 7·85 miles from Weston, was the location of the company's offices, locomotive and carriage sheds, workshops, etc. It was originally the terminus of the Weston to Clevedon section until the Portishead extension was opened in 1907. Here No. 2 *Portishead* is outside the locomotive shed in April 1936. The metal water tanks were installed in 1923.

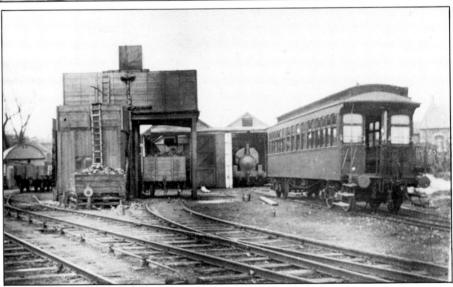

An almost identical viewpoint in 1910 shows the original wooden water tower and coaling point. *Walton Park* is in the shed. The carriage sheds were added and the track layout modified in 1920

Author's Collection

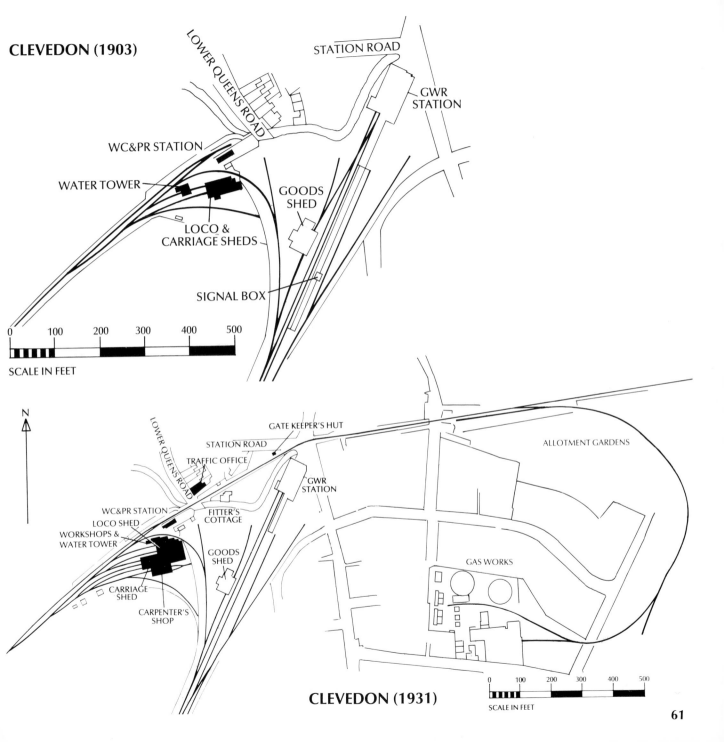

CLEVEDON (1903)

LOWER QUEENS ROAD

STATION ROAD

GWR STATION

WC&PR STATION

WATER TOWER

GOODS SHED

LOCO & CARRIAGE SHEDS

SIGNAL BOX

0   100   200   300   400   500

SCALE IN FEET

N

LOWER QUEENS ROAD

GATE KEEPER'S HUT

STATION ROAD

TRAFFIC OFFICE

GWR STATION

WC&PR STATION

LOCO SHED

FITTER'S COTTAGE

WORKSHOPS & WATER TOWER

GOODS SHED

ALLOTMENT GARDENS

CARRIAGE SHED

CARPENTER'S SHOP

GAS WORKS

CLEVEDON (1931)

0   100   200   300   400   500

SCALE IN FEET

61

Both photographs on this page were taken in 1921 and show the station building at Clevedon where the accomodation consisted of a waiting room, booking office and toilets. The upper view is looking towards Portishead and shows fitter Hill's cottage to the right of the crossing gates. The lower photograph looks towards Weston and shows the then recently constructed elevated platform with shelter and water tanks at each end. Also note the water softening plant adjacent to the original wooden covered water tanks. *E. H. Hazell*

The interior of the locomotive shed at Clevedon in 1921. Note the roof lights and ventilation canopy. The door on the right at the far end leads to fitter Hill's office. Access to the workshop is through a door on the left.

E. H. Hazell

The interior of the workshop taken in 1921 showing the forge, lathes and machinery.

E. H. Hazell

At Clevedon on Whitsun Bank Holiday
Monday 17 May 1937 with passengers waiting on the platform for the train to Weston
which is just arriving from Portishead. No. 5
with two of the original cars, 2 and 4.

Weston, Clevedon & Portishead Railway.

WHITSUN HOLIDAY SERVICE

BANK HOLIDAY,
Monday, May 29th, 1939.

The ordinary Train Service will be cancelled on the above date and the following trains will run :—

DOWN TRAINS.

		a.m.	a.m.	a.m.	a.m.	p.m.	p.m.	p.m.	p.m.	p.m.
PORTISHEAD,	dep.	—	9.5	10.15	11.30	1.10	3.5	4.15	7.30	10.5
CADBURY ROAD,	dep.	—	9.15	10.25	11.40	1.20	3.15	4.25	7.40	10.15
CLEVEDON,	dep.	8.20	9.35	10.55	12.5	2.15	3.30	4.45	8.5	10.30
WICK 'ST.' LAWRENCE,	dep.	8.35	9.50	11.10	12.20	2.30	3.45	5.0	8.20	Stops
WORLE,	dep.	8.43	9.57	11.17	12.28	2.38	3.55	5.8	8.28	
WESTON-SUPER-MARE,	arr.	8.50	10.5	11.24	12.35	2.45	4.5	5.15	8.35	

UP TRAINS.

		a.m.	a.m.	a.m.	a.m.	p.m.	p.m.	p.m.	p.m.	p.m.
WESTON-SUPER-MARE,	dep.	—	9.5	10.15	11.35	12.45	3.0	4.10	5.30	9.0
WORLE,	dep.	—	9.15	10.23	11.43	12.52	3.9	4.20	5.40	9.10
WICK ST. LAWRENCE,	dep.	—	9.27	10.31	11.51	1.0	3.17	4.28	5.48	9.18
CLEVEDON,	dep.	8.35	9.40	10.55	12.10	2.30	3.35	4.40	6.10	9.30
CADBURY ROAD,	dep.	8.45	9.50	11.5	12.20	2.40	3.48	Stops	6.23	9.43
PORTISHEAD,	arr.	8.55	10.0	11.20	12.45	2.55	4.0		6.40	10.0

All Trains stop at Intermediate Stations to pick up or set down, as required.

EXCURSION TICKETS will be issued ON ALL TRAINS as follows :—

FARE.
2nd Class Return.

Portishead and Portishead South to Weston-super-Mare	1/10
Portishead and Portishead South to Clevedon	9½d.
Portishead to Walton Park	8d.
Cadbury Road to Weston-super-Mare	1/7
Cadbury Road to Clevedon	7½d.
Walton-in-Gordano to Weston-super-Mare	1/4
Walton-in-Gordano to Clevedon	4½d.
Clevedon to Weston-super-Mare	1/1
Clevedon to Portishead South and Portishead	9½d.
Worle to Clevedon	9½d.
Worle to Portishead South and Portishead	1/7
Worle to Weston-super-Mare	3½d.
Ham Lane to Weston-super-Mare	8½d.
Wick St. Lawrence to Weston-super-Mare	6½d.
Weston-super-Mare to Walton Park	1/4
Weston-super-Mare to Clevedon	1/1
Weston-super-Mare to Portishead South and Portishead	1/10
Wick St. Lawrence to Clevedon	6½d.
Ham Lane to Clevedon	6½d.

Available day of issue only and to return by any train and subject to the conditions shewn on the Excursion Programme, dated Sept. 1938, with regard to the issue of these Tickets.   Children under 3 free, over 3 and under 14 half fare.

Traffic Office, Clevedon, May, 1939.   W. H. AUSTEN, Manager.

Scene at Clevedon taken in July 1936 from a carriage window and showing No. 5 taking on coal and No. 1 in the siding in front of the carriage shed.　*Author's Collection*

No. 2 *Portishead* with a train consisting of the ex-LSWR triplet set passing the small railcar and trailer at Clevedon on its return from Portishead. Easter Bank Holiday, 9 April 1928.

H. G. W. Household

Soon after World War I Colonel Stephens experimented with the use of concrete blocks in place of the normal sleepers. A section of track between Lower Queens Road and the Triangle at Clevedon was adopted for this purpose. The blocks were made at Clevedon and measured 20" x 12" x 7½". The rails were fastened to these blocks by spikes driven into wooden pegs which were cast into the blocks. On the section illustrated here all the original sleepers have been replaced and metal ties used on every third pair of blocks. This proved to be reasonably successful. However, the method was modified slightly by alternating two pairs of blocks with wooden sleepers. As they were of little use after the line closed many of these blocks remained in situ and in fact there are still some to be found at the present time. The track from Clevedon to Portishead was laid with flat bottomed rails weighing 60 lbs per yard in 30 feet lengths, as apposed to the slightly lighter rails of 56 lbs laid on the earlier section. *Colonel Stephens Railway Collection*

Clevedon, Station Road crossing. The gates here were one of a set of three which masked Station Road, Kenn Road and the Triangle and were operated from a shed hidden from view by the large sign on the right. When the gates were being operated a loud burglar alarm type bell, fitted to the gate across Kenn Road, sounded. 1930.

R. K. Cope

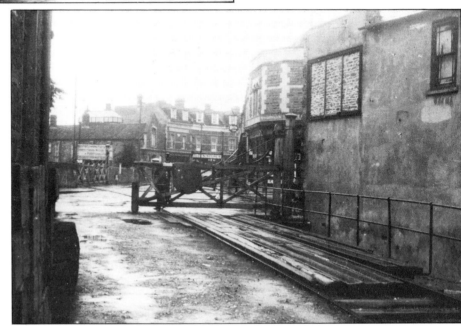

The view towards Station Road from the gap between the Constitutional Club and the Clevedon Engineering Company's premises. Note the extension arm to the crossing gate which masked the road from the Triangle. 1930. *R. K. Cope*

No. 3 *Weston* crossing Clevedon Triangle bound for Portishead. 13 July 1935.

S. W. Baker

No. 4 crossing Clevedon Triangle in September 1937.

Looking towards Clevedon East in December 1936 with the siding to the gas works off to the right. Also visible is the Parnell Road goods yard siding. The latter had a platform made up of the bases of old goods wagons.

No. 5, in September 1937, running light to the gas works to bring back a load of empties. Seen here crossing Parnell Road, Clevedon, with driver Plumley on the footplate and guard Jack Riddick standing on the locomotive steps.

This rustic scene in August 1937 shows No. 5 hauling three empties back to Clevedon station from the gas works. Most of the ground alongside the track was unfenced and opened directly onto allotments.

An official photograph taken in June 1932 by the makers, Gloucester Railway Carriage & Wagon Company Limited, of one of the Clevedon Gas Company's wagons.

Author's Collection

This photograph taken in September 1937 shows No. 1 *Clevedon* leaving the Clevedon Gas Company's yard with a load of empty wagons. Guard Dan Carey is riding on the locomotive's steps, a common practice, there being little room inside the cab.

No. 4 with a mixed train from Clevedon to Portishead seen here in April 1938 near Clevedon Saw Mills.

Taken from the 3.30 p.m. train from Clevedon to Portishead in Wednesday 22 September 1937. No. 4 and ex-Taff Vale Railway coach 18. Guard Jack Riddick is opening the gates at Clevedon East.

Clevedon East halt in December 1938 looking towards Portishead. This was the commencement of the local beauty spot known as the 'Swiss Valley'.

Clevedon All Saints halt in August 1936 looking towards Portishead. This was a complex road crossing, the line crossing All Saints Lane and the main road to Portishead at an oblique angle. Both crossings were provided with gates operated from a hut sited on a triangular area of ground midway between the two crossings. These gates were manned by the local blacksmith, Sam Harris, whose premises were immediately opposite. The halt was not opened until 1917.

No. 4 with ex-TVR coach between Clevedon East and Clevedon All Saints bound for Portishead in December 1937. Note the grass covered track. The distance from Weston-super-Mare to Clevedon East was 8·54 miles and there was a mere 300 yards further to Clevedon All Saints.

No. 4 with a Portishead to Clevedon train, consisting of the ex-LSWR close coupled set, crossing Tickenham Road, East Clevedon, in September 1937. Guard Dan Carey is opening the gates and driver Tom Gatford is on the footplate.

The large Drewry railcar bound for Portishead crossing the road at Clevedon All Saints in September 1936. Note the oblique angle of the crossing and the crossing gates reflected in the cab windows.

A local postcard of the view from Strawberry Hill, Clevedon, around the turn of the century, showing the Swiss Valley. The route of the line was approximately from the centre right passing behind the blacksmith's premises (lower centre) and along the road to the lower left of the picture.
Author's Collection

The Valley of East Clevedon.

Walton Park halt, 9·23 miles from Weston. A rustic design of building similar to that at Portishead. There was a loop to the north of the main line with an intermediate connection to the right leading off to Conygar Quarry and the stone loading bay. The remains of the latter together with approximately twenty yards of track can still be seen. For some inexplicable reason this was never removed. Conygar Quarry produced pennant stone much of which was used for ballast on the Weston section. This point is the commencement of the Gordano Valley which has now been designated a conservation area.

No. 2 *Portishead* with a mixed train bound for Portishead passing Walton Park in November 1938. The loop in the background was primarily for shunting wagons in and out of the quarry. The connection to Conygar Quarry is in the foreground. This whole area has now been developed for housing and there is little sign of the route of the original track. However further up the valley towards Walton-in-Gordano earthworks marking the line of the railway can be clearly seen.

No. 4 with a pair of the ex-Metropolitan Railway close coupled coaches heading up the Gordano Valley between Walton Park and Walton-in-Gordano, bound for Portishead in September 1937.

Walton-in-Gordano halt looking towards Portishead in October 1938. The halt served this small picturesque village in the heart of the Gordano Valley.

This photograph was taken at about the same time but a few yards further up the track towards Portishead and shows the loop and cattle pens installed in 1926. This area has changed little over the years and the route of the line is clearly visible, especially that depicted in this photograph.

W. Vaughan-Jenkins

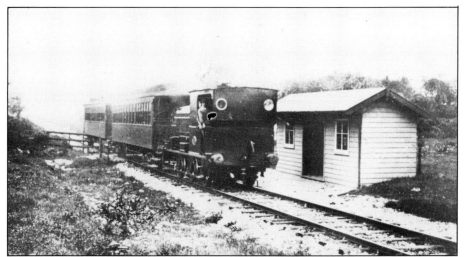

Although given the name Cadbury Road this halt was in fact at Weston-in-Gordano, the largest village in the Gordano Valley. There was a track leading from this point to Cadbury Camp, an ancient encampment on the top of the hill to the south of the valley. A siding existed on the south side of the line and was used in World War I for the distribution of horse manure, from Cavalry stables at Avonmouth, to local farmers. The halt was 11·42 miles from Weston. No. 3 *Weston* arrives with a train for Portishead on the opening day of the new extension, 7 August 1907. *Author's Collection*

Taken by a photographer of the Bristol *Evening Post* on 15 February 1936 the 10.15 a.m. from Portishead arrives at Cadbury Road headed by No. 5. *Author's Collection*

Approximately 800 yards east of Cadbury Road halt the sidings serving the Black Rock Quaries were located. The basic sidings and loading bay were installed in 1919. In 1931, due to the increase in stone traffic, a more complex system of sidings together with stone crushing and grading plant were added. These quarries were the main source of freight traffic for the WC&PR, that from the Conygar Quarry being substantially less. The Terrier locomotive No. 2 *Portishead* was known to have hauled up to thirty loaded wagons to Portishead although the average load would have been about ten wagons. The quarry owned about 75 ten or eleven ton wagons which were lined with steel plating for carrying coated roadstone. The quarries were operated by Black Rock Quarries Ltd., and were latterly a subsidiary of Roads Reconstruction (1934) Ltd. They had their own two feet narrow gauge system connecting to the concrete loading bay where small hopper or tipper wagons would discharge into the larger standard gauge wagons beneath. Motive power was by two 0-4-0 well tanks built by Hudswell Clarke and supplied in 1919. The lower photograph taken in 1921 shows one of these locomotives with three small wagons discharging their load into wagons on the siding below the loading bay. Note the Lancashire & Yorkshire Railway wagon. The upper photograph was taken from a Clevedon to Portishead train on 22 September 1937 as it approached the Black Rock Quarries. *Lower: E. H. Hazell*

Hudswell Clarke 0-4-0 well tank *Lion* and three hopper wagons at Black Rock Quarries in 1921, taken at the same time as the lower photograph on the preceding page.

E. H. Hazell

Looking towards Portishead, this view was taken from a train crossing the Portishead to Bristol road at Portishead South station on 22 September 1937. This station was 13·36 miles from Weston and only 0·65 miles short of the terminus at Portishead. Located at a distance of 12·8 miles from Weston was Clapton Road halt, the site of which now forms part of the drive to a private residence. Clapton Road served the small village of Clapton-in-Gordano, nearly one mile to the south east, and there was no shelter here.

Portishead South station, looking towards Portishead in 1937. The shelter was on the north east side of the line and trailing points led to a siding 250 feet in length, used mainly by a local coal merchant. This area is now occupied by a housing estate with an access road over the site of the station.

C. R. L. Coles

Portishead station in July 1936 looking towards Clevedon. The level crossing in the foreground shows the line leading to the connection with the GWR. The lane at this point provided the main access to Portishead High Street through an archway beneath the White Lion Inn. The lane has long disappeared and, like the site of the station, now forms part of the main arterial access to the town although the archway beneath the Inn still exists. Portishead station was 14·01 miles from Weston. The track layout consisted of a run-round loop and a further loop which ran over a weighbridge. A substantial siding connected with Mustad's nail factory, the latter surviving until 1987. There was originally no platform, passengers having to use a gravel surface at ground level, but about 1920 a platform of solid construction and only about twelve inches high was provided.

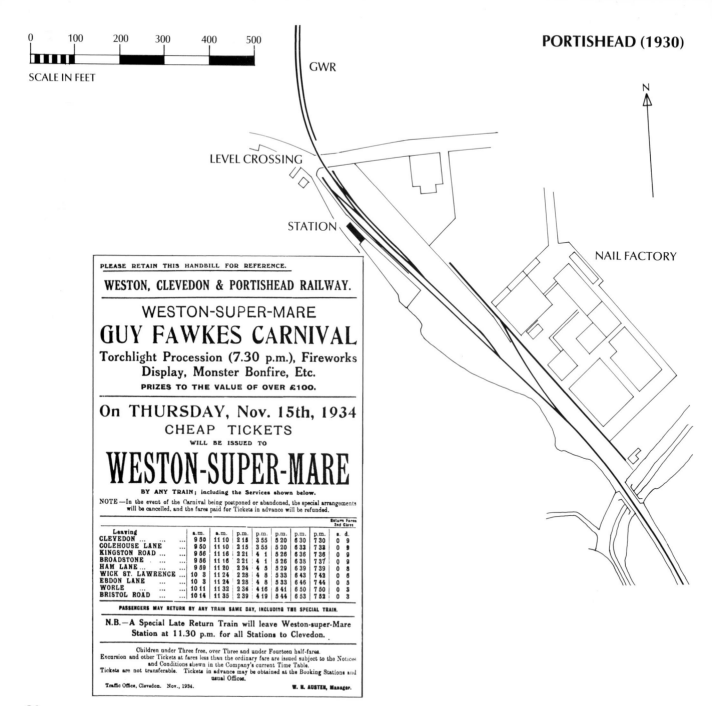

Station building at Portishead in its final form in 1921. The original building, which was later extended, was only two thirds the size of that shown. Note the rustic design. The accomodation consisted of booking office, waiting room and ladies waiting room, the last named constituting the extension which was added prior to 1912.

E. H. Hazell

Portishead station on 7 August 1907, the first day of scheduled services after the opening of the extended line. Copied from a postcard of the day it shows No. 3 *Weston* running round after arriving from Clevedon. The connection with the GWR in the foreground is not yet connected and was first used on 2 November 1908.

Author's Collection

No. 2 *Portishead* with a pair of close coupled ex-Metropolitan Railway coaches at Portishead in about 1933. *Author's Collection*

Also in about 1933, No. 5 descends the incline from the GWR at Portishead after performing shunting duties. Guard Jack Riddick on the locomotive step.
Author's Collection

A reproduction of an early commercial postcard from the days when it was fashionable to produce pictures of such 'interesting' subjects. It shows Mustad's nail factory looking towards Portishead station taken from a position just north of the bridge depicted below. *Author's Collection*

THE NAIL FACTORY. PORTISHEAD. 36.

WRIGHT'S "PICTURETTE" SERIES.

One of the few substantial remains of the WC&PR existing today photographed in 1982 looking towards the site of the old station. The steel framework of the bridge over a rhyne is virtually intact and can easily be seen from the adjoining road which leads into Portishead town centre from Bristol and Portbury.

ACCIDENTS

A photograph taken by the local press following an accident at Wick St. Lawrence on 5 April 1934. A small bridge over a rhyne has collapsed under the weight of the *Hesperus* and the railway staff are in the process of rescuing the locomotive, which was shunting wagons on the jetty at the time. The figure on the left is that of the chief fitter, Alf Hill, who was supervising the work.

Author's Collection

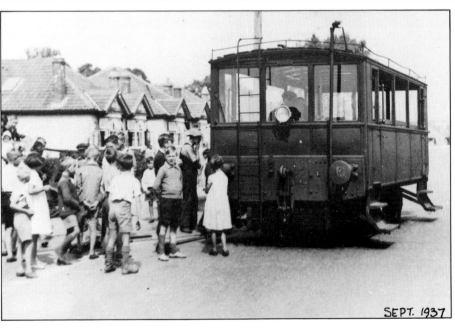

The *Western Daily Press* took this photograph which shows the small railcar after a collision with a brewers van on the Locking Road crossing in September 1937. This photograph must have been taken soon after the incident as 'shocked' passengers are still seated in the vehicle.

Author's Collection

These two photographs were taken by Mr H. G. W. Household on 13 July 1927 and show the aftermath of the derailment of the ex-GER four wheeled brake van, no. 14, at Worle Town. The upper photograph shows the van being righted and the lower shows its load of milk churns being transferred to the Cranes open wagon to be towed back to Clevedon behind the small railcar. After this incident the brake van was transferred to the dump siding at Clevedon where it remained until it was scrapped in 1940 after the railway closed.

There were a number of accidents during the operational life of the line, some involving fatalities. These occurred mainly at level crossings and the most serious was that at Worle in 1903 which has been referred to earlier.
H. G. W. Household

A collection of company's tickets reproduced here by courtesy of Mr Victor Ware. Mr Ware worked on the line during the latter years, first as office boy and then as station agent at Portishead. The tickets shown here were the type in use at the time of closure and differed from those in use in the early days. When the line was operating as a tramway the tickets were printed with the different destinations, the conductor cutting the ticket below the name of the destination. He would retain the lower portion as a credit which he would hand in with his money at the end of the day.

Company button.

WESTON, CLEVEDON & PORTISHEAD RAILWAY.

SECOND CLASS FREE PASS No. 9

Expiring unless previously recalled *31st December* 1936

Pass Mr *D. H. Robertson*

between *all Stations*

NOT TRANSFERABLE.

Signature of Holder *D H Roberts*

The holder of this Pass may also be required to give a specimen signature.

This Pass must be produced for examination when called for by the Officers of the Company, and upon the day of expiry must be returned to General Manager's Office, Tonbridge, Kent.

The Holder is subject to the same Rules and Regulations as other Passengers.

This Pass is granted upon the understanding that it is to be taken as evidence of an agreement that the Company over whose lines it is available are not to be held liable for any pecuniary or other responsibility to the Holder for loss of life, personal injury or delay, or for loss of or delay or damage to property however caused, that may be sustained by such person while using the Pass.　　　　W. H. AUSTEN,
　　　　　　　　　　　　　　　General Manager.

Issued by ....

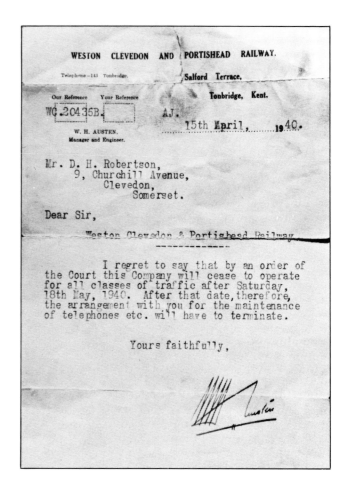

WESTON CLEVEDON AND PORTISHEAD RAILWAY.

Telephone—143 Tonbridge.　　Salford Terrace,

Our Reference　Your Reference　　Tonbridge, Kent.

WC.20436B.　　　　AJ.

W. H. AUSTEN,　　　　15th April, 1940.
Manager and Engineer.

Mr. D. H. Robertson,
　9, Churchill Avenue,
　　Clevedon,
　　　Somerset.

Dear Sir,

　　Weston Clevedon & Portishead Railway

　　　I regret to say that by an order of the Court this Company will cease to operate for all classes of traffic after Saturday, 18th May, 1940. After that date, therefore, the arrangement with you for the maintenance of telephones etc. will have to terminate.

　　　Yours faithfully,

Mr D. H. Robinson was employed by the company as an outside contractor. He had an electrical business in premises at the bottom of Chapel Hill, Clevedon, and signed a contract with the WC&PR on 31 December 1934 to maintain all telephones and electrical equipment 'throughout the Company's system', including the electrical equipment at the Kenn Road crossing gates. The letter on the right, signed by W. H. Austen, terminates this contract after the line's closure on 18 May 1940.

FINALE

The last day of scheduled services. No. 4
with cars 2 and 4 is the last train to arrive at
Weston on 18 May 1940

WESTON, CLEVEDON & PORTISHEAD RLY

General Manager's Office,

W.C.   7th May, 1940.

SALFORD TERRACE,

TONBRIDGE, KENT

<u>Closing of Railway.</u>

In view of the closing of this railway for all classes
of traffic, I very much regret to say that your services will not be
required after Wednesday, 15th May, 1940.

Mr. V. G. Ware,
        Cypress Cottage,
                Tickenham Road,
                        Clevedon, Somerset.

WESTON, CLEVEDON & PORTISHEAD RLY.

GENERAL MANAGER.

W. H. Austen's letter to Vic Ware terminating his services with the company.
Courtesy V. A. Ware

18 May 1940. The last train leaves Weston for Clevedon.   *Alan Ball*

Notice on the booking office window at Clevedon.   *H. C. Casserley*

The scene from Yeo Bridge in June 1943 showing the track removed in the direction of Clevedon.